D0903621

BRITAIN IN PICTURES

THE BRITISH PEOPLE IN PICTURES

BRITISH RAILWAYS

GENERAL EDITOR
W. J. TURNER

BRITISH RAILWAYS

ARTHUR ELTON

WITH
8 PLATES IN COLOUR
AND
32 ILLUSTRATIONS IN
BLACK & WHITE

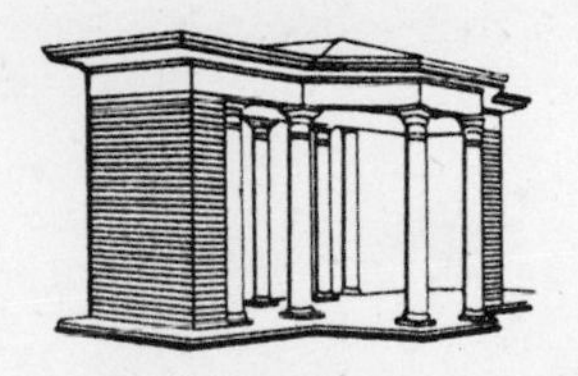

COLLINS · 14 ST. JAMES'S PLACE · LONDON
MCMXLVII

PRODUCED BY
ADPRINT LIMITED LONDON

FIRST PUBLISHED 1945
SECOND IMPRESSION (REVISED) 1947

PRINTED IN GREAT BRITAIN BY
CLARKE & SHERWELL LTD NORTHAMPTON
ON MELLOTEX BOOK PAPER MADE BY
TULLIS RUSSELL & CO LTD MARKINCH SCOTLAND

LIST OF ILLUSTRATIONS

PLATES IN COLOUR

THE TANFIELD ARCH IN 1804
Aquatint printed in colours. I. C. Stadler after J. Atkinson, 1804

TRAVELLING ON THE LIVERPOOL AND MANCHESTER RAILWAY
Aquatint coloured by hand. S. G. Hughes after I. Shaw, 1831

OLIVE MOUNT CUTTING ON THE LIVERPOOL AND MANCHESTER RAILWAY
Aquatint coloured by hand. Drawn and engraved by T. T. Bury, 1831
From *Six Views of the Liverpool and Manchester Railway*

THIRD CLASS TRAVEL c. 1845
Lithograph printed in colours
From Frank Musgrave's *The Excursion Train Galop* [1862]

THE ATMOSPHERIC RAILWAY AT DAWLISH, 1847
Unsigned water colour

THE METROPOLITAN RAILWAY NEAR PADDINGTON, 1863
Lithograph printed in colours

CANNON STREET STATION c. 1900
Illustration by Marcus from an unidentified periodical

CAMDEN TOWN ENGINE SHEDS, c. 1935
L.M.S. poster by Norman Wilkinson

BLACK AND WHITE ILLUSTRATIONS

PAGE

A LOCOMOTIVE BY HAWTHORNE, c. 1835
Pen and ink drawing (cover design)

A SIGNALMAN ON THE LONDON AND BIRMINGHAM RAILWAY, 1838 — 5
Pen and ink drawing by Mary Elizabeth Elton

RALPH ALLEN'S WAGGONWAY NEAR BATH — 7
Engraving in line by Anthony Walker, 1750

THE PENRHYN RAILWAY, 1803 — 9
Repertory of Arts and Manufactures Vol. III (2nd series)

A NEWCASTLE CHALDRON, 1764 — 11
The London Magazine. Vol. XXXIII

RICHARD TREVITHICK, 1771-1833 — 13
Oil painting by John Linnell
By courtesy of the Science Museum

A BLENKINSOP LOCOMOTIVE AT A YORKSHIRE COLLIERY, 1814 — 14
Aquatint. R. & D. Havell after G. Walker
The Costume of Yorkshire. G. Walker, 1814

PROBABLE DESIGN OF TREVITHICK'S FIRST LOCOMOTIVE — 15
Timothy Hackworth and the Locomotive, Robert Young, 1923
By courtesy of The Locomotive Publishing Co.

PASSENGER TRAFFIC ON THE STOCKTON AND DARLINGTON RAILWAY, 1826 — 17
Durham County Advertiser, October 14th, 1826. Reproduced from Dendy Marshall's *Centenary History of The Liverpool and Manchester Railway*

BRANDRETH'S PATENT 'CYCLOPEDE' — 18
History and Progress of the Steam Engine. Elijah Galloway, 1829

THE RAINHILL COMPETITORS — 19
Rocket; Sans Pareil; Novelty. Engravings in line from *The Mechanics' Magazine*, 1829. *Perseverance*. Lithograph in the Dollfus collection reproduced from a photograph in the Dendy Marshall collection

GEORGE STEPHENSON, 1781-1848 — 21
Mezzotint. T. L. Atkinson after John Lucas

NOVELTY AND TRAIN — 22
From a drawing by John Ericsson reproduced in *The Life of John Ericsson*. W. C. Church, 1890

NORTH STAR AND TRAIN — 23
From a printed handkerchief

PAGE

TRING CUTTING, JUNE 17th, 1837 — 26
Drawn and lithographed by John C. Bourne
The London and Birmingham Railway, 1839

PUMPS FOR DRAINING THE KILSBY TUNNEL — 27
Drawn and lithographed by John C. Bourne
The London and Birmingham Railway, 1839

BATH STATION — 28
Drawn and lithographed by John C. Bourne
The History . . . of The Great Western Railway, 1846

ENTRANCE TO LOCOMOTIVE ENGINE HOUSE CAMDEN TOWN — 29
Drawn and lithographed by John C. Bourne
The London and Birmingham Railway, 1839

"MIND YOUR POINTS" — 31
Illustration by John Gilbert in *The British Workman*, 1867

QUEEN VICTORIA, THE PRINCE CONSORT AND LOUIS PHILIPPE IN THE ROYAL CARRIAGE, 1844 — 35
Lithograph

THE GREAT RAILWAY GUY OF 1849 — 36
By courtesy of the Proprietors of Punch

THE RAILWAY KING — 37
A Railway Raillery. Alfred Crowquill, 1849

THE METROPOLITAN RAILWAY, 1872 — 39
London. Gustave Doré and Blanchard Jerrold, 1872

ON THE CONTINENT — 40
From an unidentified nineteenth century pencil drawing

THE ARRIVAL PLATFORM AT VICTORIA STATION — 43
Oil painting by James Tissot
By courtesy of The Leicester Galleries, London

THE FORTH BRIDGE — 44
Picture woven in silk by Thomas Stevens of Coventry

LONDON & NORTH WESTERN RAILWAY EXPRESS, c. 1913 — 45
Picture woven in silk by Thomas Stevens of Coventry

MAIN LINE — 47
Cover design of *The Railway Handbook* 1939-1940
By courtesy of The Railway Publishing Co.

LOCOMOTIVE ON THE STOCKTON AND DARLINGTON RAILWAY, 1825 — 48
Picture woven in silk by Thomas Stevens of Coventry

Ralph Allen's Waggonway near Bath
Engraving in line by Anthony Walker, 1750

BEFORE STEAM

FROM earliest times to the beginning of the nineteenth century the quantity of goods that could be carried overland was limited by the strength of a team of horses or bullocks. The greatest speed a man could reach was the speed of a horse. Animal power was sufficient in its time, when people lived mainly in small self-supporting communities. Only when loads were heavy and there was much to be moved was it necessary to have something better than a horse and cart and a rough track. So the first railways in Europe were laid down in mines, and the first known descriptions of them are in German books of mining of the sixteenth century, for at that time the mines of central and Eastern Europe were the industrial centre of the world. Though these early railways had rails made of wood, the waggons that ran on them often had flanged wooden wheels, or were kept to the lines in other ways. That is, they were true railways in the sense defined by C. F. Dendy Marshall in his *A History of British Railways down to the Year* 1830: "The conception 'railway' contains three elements: (1) the wheel, (2) a prepared track, (3) means for lateral constraint of the motion."

From the seventeenth century, the centre of mining gradually moved from Europe to Britain. This happened mainly because of a change in the technique of smelting. For centuries, metallic ores had been smelted by charcoal, made from trees in the forests bordering the mines. By the beginning of the eighteenth century many of the forests had been cut down and charcoal was becoming scarce and expensive. It was necessary to find a substitute.

After many difficulties and much experimenting, ways were found of using coke made from coal instead of charcoal made from wood. Since large quantities of coal or coke could not be transported for great distances overland, smelting could only be carried on in places where metallic ores and coal were found close together, or where transport by water was easy. For this reason, more than for any other, Britain gradually became the industrial centre of the world. Moreover, smelting with coke was more efficient than smelting with charcoal, and the output of metal increased. The mines of South Wales, Cumberland, Northumberland and Durham were opened up and flourished. European mines declined. Their railways remained primitive or died out altogether, while in Britain they were improved and multiplied. By the middle of the eighteenth century wooden railways linked the mines of Durham and Northumberland to the Tyne and to the coast, bringing coal to the water's edge for transport by sea to wherever it was wanted. Others were laid down in Shropshire, connecting the mines with the Severn, and there was even one in South Wales which used waggons propelled by sails.

As the mines near the coast or rivers became exhausted, the railways were extended inland. The lengthening of the railways brought engineering problems which have faced railway builders ever since. For the waggonways, no less than the main lines of to-day, had to have gentle gradients. Valleys had to be crossed by embankments, and rivers by bridges. Hills had to be pierced by cuttings and tunnels. The first of many great railway bridges was the Tanfield Arch in Durham. It was built in 1726, and has a span of over a hundred feet across the Beckley Burn. It was one of the wonders of the countryside, and still stands to-day, a monument to the skill and enterprise of its builder, a local mason called Ralph Wood. Though the Tanfield Arch had fallen into disuse by the end of the eighteenth century, an embankment near it, one hundred feet high and three hundred feet broad at its base, has been used for a railway ever since it was made, more than two hundred years ago.

Railways seem to have been used only in mines till Ralph Allen (1694-1764) of Prior Park, Bath, laid one in about 1730 to bring stone from his quarries on Combe Down to the city, then being built by John Wood. This was the first British railway to be minutely described and illustrated, in Volume I of Desagulier's *A Course of Experimental Philosophy*, published in 1734.

So the railways spread. Self-acting inclines on which loaded waggons running downhill pulled empty waggons up to the top were introduced. Waggon wheels were made of iron. Different kinds of brake were invented. Wooden rails were made more durable by facing them with strips of iron.

THE TANFIELD ARCH IN 1804
Aquatint printed in colours. I. C. Stadler after J. Atkinson

TRAVELLING ON THE LIVERPOOL AND MANCHESTER RAILWAY
Aquatint coloured by hand. S. G. Hughes after I. Shaw, 1831

Rails made wholly of cast iron were first used in about 1789, wrought iron rails in about 1810. Rails supported by chairs something in the style familiar to-day were designed as early as 1797.

As well as the familiar kind of railway with waggons with flanged wheels, there were also plateways. These had rails of right-angled section, thus:—L, and the wheels of the waggons which ran on them had no flanges. They were kept to the track by a flange on the rails instead of on the wheels. Plateways were built fairly widely in the early nineteenth century because waggons for them could also run on an ordinary road, but the disadvantage of dirt and stones accumulating in the angle of the plates led to their gradual abandonment, and few steam locomotives were built for them. The first railway in London—The Surrey Iron Railway—opened in 1805, was a plateway. Sir Richard Phillips in his *A Morning's Walk to Kew*, published in *The Monthly Magazine* in 1814, described it thus:

> "The manufactories of Wandsworth are created or greatly aided by the pure stream of the Wandle, and by the Surrey iron rail-way, which runs from Croydon to a spacious and busy wharf, on the Thames . . . I felt renewed delight on witnessing at this place the economy of horse-labour on the iron rail-way; and a heavy sigh escaped me, as I thought of the inconceivable millions which had been spent about Malta, four or five of which might have been the means of extending *double lines of iron rail-ways* from London to Edinburgh, Glasgow, Holyhead, Milford, Falmouth, Yarmouth, Dover, and Portsmouth! . . . We might, ere this, have witnessed our mail coaches running at the rate of ten miles an hour, drawn by a single horse, or impelled fifteen miles by Blenkinsop's steam engine! Such would have been a legitimate motive for overstepping the income of the nation, and the completion of so great and useful a work would have afforded *rational* grounds for public triumph in a general jubilee!"

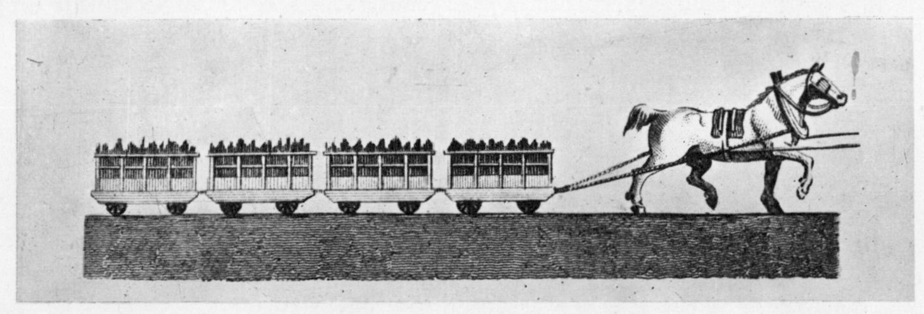

THE PENRHYN RAILWAY, 1803

THE LOCOMOTIVE

THE first practical steam engine—a stationary engine for pumping—was designed and built by a Cornishman, Thomas Newcomen (1663-1729) in 1712. Newcomen's engines were first used mainly in Cornwall where draining the tin and copper mines was becoming more difficult each year. For this reason, Cornwall led the world in the use of the steam engine. When James Watt (1736-1819) patented a fundamental improvement to Newcomen's engine in 1769 by which the volume of water raised for a given consumption of coal—all imported into Cornwall by sea from Wales—was greatly increased, scores of Watt engines were built all over the county. Skilled erectors and mechanics came to the West from all parts of Britain.

Though James Watt was one of the greatest mechanical engineers that has ever lived, his work was characteristic of his time, and his engines were heavy, cumbersome and slow. To drive them he used, not the direct pressure of steam, but the weight of the atmosphere. That is, he used steam to create a vacuum underneath the piston, which was then forced to the bottom of the cylinder by the weight of the air. This kind of engine was too heavy and too slow-moving to be used to drive a self-propelled steam carriage or locomotive.

The first self-moving steam engine in Britain, and one of the first in the world, was made, not by Watt, but by his principal engine erector in Cornwall, William Murdock (1754-1839), the son of an Ayrshire miller and farmer. (The Frenchman, Nicholas Cugnot (1725-1804) built a steam carriage in Paris in 1769. His work was isolated, and his invention came to nothing.) Murdock anticipated the ideas of the nineteenth century. He made machines and models which were delicate and fast moving. He used the pressure of steam directly. His work was very different from that of his master, who opposed his new ideas. For James Watt, with all his brilliance, was a mean employer and extremely conservative.

The first mention of Murdock's interest in a locomotive steam engine is in a letter, dated March 7th, 1784, from Watt's agent in Cornwall to Watt:

> "He [Murdock] has got an amazing genius and I am almost afraid will lead him too far. He has mentioned to me a new scheme which you may be assured he is very interested upon but which he is afraid of mentioning to you for fear of you laughing at him, it is no less than drawing carriages upon the Road with Steam Engines. . . He says that what he proposes, is different from anything you ever thought of, and that he is positively certain of its answering and that there is a great deal of Money to be made by it."

Watt thought the idea a waste of time, and Murdock seems to have dropped it till 1786, when Watt's agent wrote on August 9th: "Mr. Murdock

A NEWCASTLE CHALDRON, 1764

desires me to inform you that he has made a small engine . . . that he has applyed to a small Carriage which answers amazingly." On September 2nd Watt's partner, Matthew Boulton, described what appears to have been another model :

> "He hath made travel [a model carriage] a mile or two in River's great room in a circle, making it carry the fire shovel, poker and tongs. I think it fortunate that I met him, as I am persuaded I can either cure him of the disorder, or turn the evil to good."

Murdock made a number of models, but was persuaded—or even compelled—to give up working on them in about 1791, and it is unlikely that he ever made a full scale steam carriage. Though Watt was narrow minded and jealous, it is probable that a practical steam carriage could not have been made at this time. Even if the theoretical problems could have been overcome, eighteenth century craftsmanship would not have been fine enough for the light and accurate construction necessary, and a safe high-pressure boiler could not have been made much before 1800. One of Murdock's models has been preserved in the Boulton and Watt collection at Birmingham.

Richard Trevithick (1771-1833), the son of one of Watt's principal rivals in Cornwall, made a full size steam road carriage in 1801. Almost as soon as he had finished building it he left it to get up steam while he went to have a drink. When he got back the boiler was empty and red hot and the carriage was destroyed. Trevithick probably made another in 1803 which he may have driven from Paddington to Islington. And in 1804 he made the first locomotive in the world to run on rails. This started work on Monday, February 13th, 1804, on the Penydarren tramroad, near Merthyr Tydfil. A week later it pulled ten tons of bar-iron from the Penydarren ironworks to the Glamorganshire Canal, nine miles away. As well as the iron it hauled seventy sightseers, "drawn thither (as well as many hundreds of others) by invincible curiosity."

The Penydarren tramway was a plateway, so the wheels of Trevithick's engine would have had no flanges, and it could have run on a road if it had had steering gear. Its boiler was about five feet long. Its cylinder was probably horizontal and on top of the boiler. It had a flywheel, and the running wheels were driven by a train of gears.

Trevithick was mercurial, erratic and unbusinesslike. By rights he should have been the first of the successful British locomotive engineers. Instead, after the Penydarren engine, which failed, perhaps because it was too heavy for the plates, he seems to have made only two more, one for the Wylam Colliery near Newcastle-upon-Tyne, which probably never started work at all, and one named "catch me who can," which was exhibited on a circular track near Euston in 1808. Even this does not seem to have attracted much attention, and Trevithick gave up locomotive work for good.

The locomotive was not an isolated invention. It could not have been successful, for example, until engineers and manufacturers had found ways of rolling plates for high pressure boilers, and until accurate machine tools had been designed, and men trained to use them. In fact, it was a firm of engineers and machine tool makers, Fenton, Murray and Wood of Leeds, which took up the locomotive after Trevithick. The firm was celebrated all over the country and was one of the principal rivals of Boulton and Watt. In 1811 or 1812 Matthew Murray (1765?-1826) and John Blenkinsop (1783-1831), a viewer of the Middleton colliery, Leeds, designed and built a locomotive. It was driven by a gear wheel meshing with a toothed rack laid beside the rails, an idea patented by Blenkinsop in 1811, since he thought that the smooth driving wheels would not grip the rails. Six Blenkinsop locomotives were built and put to work in 1812 and 1813. Their design was influenced by Trevithick's ideas.

At first the locomotive was regarded simply as a better kind of horse able to work without rest. So strong, indeed, was the identification of the horse and the locomotive that the latter was soon given living qualities in popular mythology—a romantic idea which has never been wholly lost. One of the earliest locomotives, built at Whitehaven, was named *Iron Horse*, and another, made by Blenkinsop for a Wigan colliery, was described thus:

> "The people in the neighbourhood emphatically call it 'the Walking Horse;' and, certainly . . ., it bears no little resemblance to a living animal . . . The superabundant steam is emitted at each stroke with a noise

RICHARD TREVITHICK, 1771-1833

something similar to the hard breathing or snorting of a horse—the escaping steam representing the breath of his nostrils, and the deception altogether aided by the regular motion of the engine-beam . . ."

From this time locomotives were introduced gradually. The engineer who, more than any other before George Stephenson, made the locomotive a practical success was William Hedley (1779-1843). Timothy Hackworth, who later became a famous locomotive builder, assisted him. Their first engine, built in 1811 or 1812 at Wylam, was a failure, but the next three,

A Blenkinsop Locomotive at a Yorkshire Colliery, 1814

built in 1813, were successful. Instead of following the ideas of Trevithick and Blenkinsop, these engines followed the design of stationary engines, and had complicated upper works. For this reason, and in spite of their success, their type was not perpetuated. At first, Hedley's engines probably had four wheels. They were modified to run on eight, and were changed back to four wheels again. Two Hedley locomotives, the *Puffing Billy* and the *Wylam Dilly*, the earliest to have been preserved, are in the Science Museum and at Edinburgh respectively.

George Stephenson (1781-1848), because of the partiality of his biographer, Samuel Smiles, is supposed by many people to have invented the locomotive and even railways. Even the Epitome of *The Dictionary of National Biography* describes him as the "inventor and founder" of railways. Yet Stephenson comes relatively late in the list of pioneers. Trevithick, Murray and Blenkinsop, Hedley and Hackworth, Chapman, Brunton (who made two locomotives in 1813 which pushed themselves along with mechanical legs), Stewart, and Swainson all made more or less successful engines before Stephenson's first was put to work, at the Killingworth Colliery, near Newcastle, in 1814. The early Stephenson engines were in the tradition of Trevithick. They had vertical cylinders embedded in the top of the boiler. Their four running wheels were coupled together by an endless chain running over sprocket wheels. Stephenson's abilities as a mechanical engineer have been overrated. He was a very great and imaginative *civil* engineer. He was also a forceful and resourceful businessman and negotiator. Though he did not make any fundamental contributions to the design of the locomotive, he, his son, Robert (1803-1859), and his colleagues are largely responsible for perfecting the locomotive and for making the passenger railway an economic success.

George and Robert Stephenson gradually brought in improvements. They put coupling rods between the engine wheels and did away with the chain. They introduced springs, eccentrics (first invented by Murdock) to work the valves, and tubular boilers. In 1828, Robert persuaded his father to put the cylinders on the side of the boiler instead of on top of it, and thus began to move them towards their final position. The locomotive gradually became something not unlike the machine we know to-day.

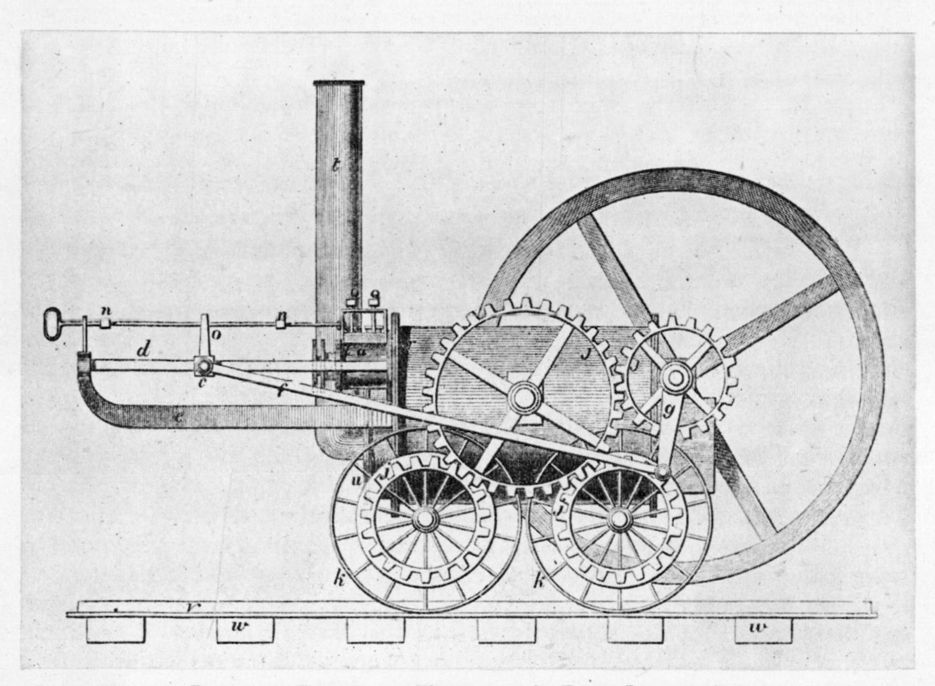

PROBABLE DESIGN OF TREVITHICK'S FIRST LOCOMOTIVE

THE FIRST PUBLIC RAILWAY

THE British Railway system was part of a process greater than itself. It was the result of economic changes which had been going on at least since the beginning of the eighteenth century, changes from cottage industry by family groups, using simple tools and simple man-driven machines such as the lathe and the loom, to factory industry by wage earners, using power-driven machinery.

The simple ways were given up for a number of reasons. Theories of chemistry as old as Aristotle were breaking down as new elements and compounds were discovered, and gases isolated and identified. Trade with Africa, India and America brought new materials, such as cotton and tobacco, to British ports. The trading and business classes were increasing. The demand for all kinds of goods began to increase too, and a re-arrangement of industrial methods became necessary. Factories began to be built. Workers had to live near the factories. New towns were built to house them. Agriculture had to be reformed to supply, not only the needs of those who worked on the land and their neighbours, but the bulk needs of the growing towns. The enclosure acts—we should say to-day—"rationalised" work on the land, and drove many countrymen to work in the mills.

The first factories were usually driven by water power and were built along the banks of rivers. Their output had to be relatively large to cover overheads and to ensure a profit. So goods had to be sent to distant markets for sale, and a better transport system became essential. By the end of the eighteenth century many cities were connected to each other or to the sea by canals, but canals alone could not solve the transport difficulties, for they could be built only in suitable country and had to be supplied with water. They suffered from drought and frost, and they were slow.

The output of the mills and manufactories went on rising as new machines were invented and new processes developed. In 1782, James Watt adapted his steam engine, hitherto used only for pumping, to supply power for factories. Within a few years his 'rotative' engines freed factories from the uncertainties of water power, but the need for coal, and the difficulty of transporting it except by water, still limited the sites where they could be built. In 1805 William Murdock and Samuel Clegg helped to increase production yet further by applying gas lighting to the mills. Work could go on through the dark winter evenings far into the night.

By the eighteen-twenties transport difficulties had become intolerable. The only possible answer was the steam railway. The first public railway to be designed from the beginning to use locomotives as well as horses was The Stockton and Darlington, opened in 1825. Passengers were horse-drawn for the first few years (a practice introduced by The Oystermouth Railway, near Swansea, in 1807) and the engines were confined to goods traffic. But the first public railway, in the modern sense of the term, was The

OLIVE MOUNT CUTTING ON THE LIVERPOOL AND MANCHESTER RAILWAY
Aquatint coloured by hand. Drawn and engraved by T. T. Bury, 1831

THIRD CLASS TRAVEL, c. 1845
Lithograph printed in colours

Liverpool and Manchester Railway, opened in 1830. It was built in competition with the Bridgewater Canal, opened in 1772, which had become inadequate for the traffic and which charged very high tolls. Sometimes, it was said, it was quicker to bring goods from America to Liverpool than it was to move them by canal from Liverpool to Manchester.

The Liverpool and Manchester Railway was violently opposed, and every vested interest was up in arms. People with money in the turnpike roads. Coach proprietors. Coach builders. Saddle and harness makers. Landowners who claimed that the steam engine would lower the value of their land, ruin their farms by frightening the cattle, and destroy the amenities of their estates and parks. Shopkeepers who thought that rail making would cause a run on iron which would send up its price and ruin the blacksmith and the ironmonger. Those who did not attack, ridiculed.

In spite of opposition the Liverpool and Manchester Railway Company was founded in 1824, and applied to Parliament for a Bill in 1825. The Committee stage lasted three months and the Bill was thrown out. Thomas Creevey, who was on the committee, and who should therefore have been impartial, did everything he could to hamper its progress :

> "Sefton and I have come to the conclusion"—he wrote—"that our Ferguson is *insane*. He quite foamed at the mouth with rage in our Railway Committee in support of this infernal nuisance—the loco-motive Monster, carrying *eighty tons* of goods, and navigated by a tail of smoke and sulphur, coming thro' every man's grounds between Manchester and Liverpool . . ."

When the Bill was thrown out a few days later he wrote, "Well—this devil of a railway is strangled at last," but the company immediately drew up a new Bill, which passed through both houses in 1826. To placate opposition, the route was altered, and in consequence the engineering works were much heavier than they might have been. The approach to Liverpool was through a cutting nearly two miles long and in places more than one hundred feet deep. There was a tunnel more than a mile long, through which locomotives were at first forbidden to travel, and which was lighted by gas. A nine-arch viaduct seventy feet above the water carried the railway across the Sankey Valley. There were sixty-three bridges over or under the line. Finally, the railway had to cross Chat Moss, a quagmire which had not altered much since the time of Defoe, who had written a hundred years earlier, "The surface, at a distance looks black and dirty, and is indeed frightful to think of, for it will bear neither Horse nor Man, unless an exceedingly dry Season, and then so as not to be travelled on with Safety."

George Stephenson, after experience with colliery locomotives and on The Stockton and Darlington Railway, was appointed engineer to The Liverpool and Manchester Railway in 1826. He was in charge, not only of the building of the railway, but of the locomotive power as well. At first the directors of the railway did not know whether to use stationary engines which would pull the trains along by ropes, or locomotive engines. In order to decide, they offered a prize of £500 for a locomotive engine "which shall be a decided improvement on those now in use, as respects the consumption of smoke, increased speed, adequate power and moderate weight." There were five entries, *Rocket* built by George and Robert Stephenson, *Sans Pareil* by Timothy Hackworth, now Engine Superintendent of The Stockton and Darlington Railway, *Novelty* by Braithwaite and Ericsson, *Perseverance* by Timothy Burstall, and a contraption called

BRANDRETH'S PATENT 'CYCLOPEDE'

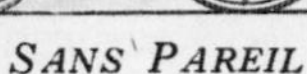

SANS PAREIL

NOVELTY

ROCKET

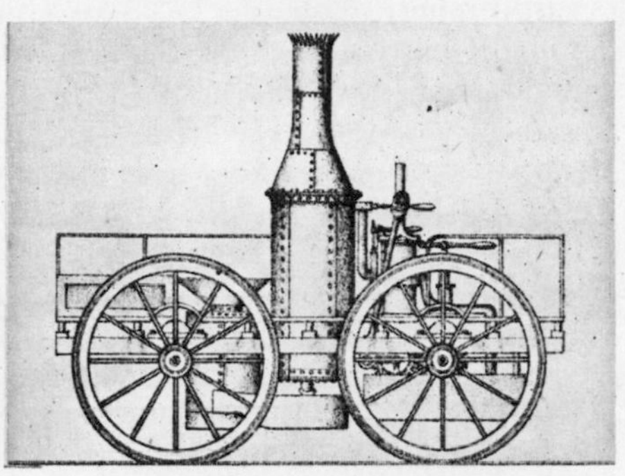

PERSEVERANCE

'*Cyclopede*' designed by T. S. Brandreth, one of the directors, and driven by a horse working a kind of treadmill.

The first day of the competition was Tuesday, October 6th, 1829. It was held on a level stretch of railway at Rainhill, about nine miles from Liverpool. There was a grandstand. Two hundred men acted as special constables and there was a crowd of at least ten thousand.

Rocket and *Novelty* reached a speed of about thirty miles an hour and caused great excitement. An eye-witness wrote of the former:

> "It seemed indeed to fly, presenting one of the most sublime spectacles of mechanical ingenuity and human daring the world ever beheld. It actually made one giddy to look at it, and filled the breasts of thousands with lively fears for the safety of the individuals who were on it, and who seemed not to run along the earth, but to fly, as it were, 'on the wings of wind.'"

George Stephenson overcame all difficulties by his skill and his persistence. The railway cost over eight hundred thousand pounds to build and was ready for work by August, 1830. In that month, and before it was opened to the public, Fanny Kemble was taken over the line. She wrote a long letter describing her trip :

"We were introduced to the little engine which was to drag us along the rails. She (for they make these curious little fire-horses all mares) consisted of a boiler, a stove, a small platform, a bench, and behind the bench a barrel containing enough water to prevent her being thirsty for fifteen miles. . . She goes upon two wheels, which are her feet, and are moved by bright steel legs called pistons; these are propelled by steam, and in proportion as more steam is applied to the upper extremities (the hip-joints, I suppose) of these pistons, the faster they move the wheels. . . The reins, bit, and bridle of this wonderful beast is a small steel handle, which applies or withdraws the steam from its legs or pistons, so that a child might manage it. . . This snorting little animal, which I felt rather inclined to pat, was then harnessed to our carriage, and, Mr. Stephenson having taken me on the bench of the engine with him, we started at about ten miles an hour. . . You can't imagine how strange it seemed to be journeying on thus, without any visible cause of progress other than the magical machine, with its flying white breath and rhythmical, unvarying pace, between . . . rocky walls. . . Bridges were thrown from side to side across the top of these cliffs, and the people looking down upon us from them seemed like pigmies standing in the sky. . .

Now for a word or two about the master [George Stephenson] of all these marvels, with whom I am most horribly in love. He is a man of from fifty to fifty-five years of age; his face is fine, though careworn, and bears an expression of deep thoughtfulness; his mode of explaining his ideas is peculiar and very original, striking, and forcible; and although his accent indicates strongly his north-country birth, his language has not the slightest touch of vulgarity or coarseness. He has certainly turned my head."

The railway was opened formally on September 15th, 1830. Eight trains started from Liverpool with a load of about eight hundred people. The principal guests, who included the Duke of Wellington, travelled in the first train. According to a contemporary account, the state carriage "was imposing, and its workmanship was perfect and tasteful; superb Grecian scrolls and balustrades, richly gilt, supported a massy handrail running round the carriage . . . The drapery was of rich crimson cloth, and the whole was surmounted by the Ducal coronet . . ." Half way there was a stop. William Huskisson, the economist, got out and was cut down by a passing engine and killed. Fanny Kemble described the day's celebrations and tragedy in detail :

"The most intense curiosity and excitement prevailed, and, though the weather was uncertain, enormous masses of densely packed people lined the road, shouting and waving hats and handkerchiefs as we flew

George Stephenson, 1781-1848

by them. What with the sight and sound of these cheering multitudes and the tremendous velocity with which we were borne past them, my spirits rose to the true champaigne height, and I never enjoyed anything so much as the first hour of our progress. . .

[My mother joined] me when I was at the height of my ecstasy, which was considerably damped by finding that she was frightened to death, and intent upon nothing but devising means of escaping from a situation which appeared to her to threaten with instant annihilation herself and all her travelling companions. . . [Shortly afterwards] a man flew by us, calling out through a speaking-trumpet to stop the engine, for that somebody in the directors' carriage had sustained an injury. We were all stopped accordingly, and presently a hundred voices were heard exclaiming that Mr. Huskisson was killed; the confusion that ensued is indescribable: the calling out from carriage to carriage to ascertain the truth . . ., the hundred questions eagerly uttered at once, and the repeated and urgent demands for surgical assistance, created a sudden turmoil that was quite sickening. At last we distinctly ascertained that the unfortunate man's thigh was broken. From Lady W [ellington] . . . I had the following details . . . The engine had stopped to take in a supply of water, and several of the gentlemen in the directors' carriage had jumped out to look about them . . . when an engine on the other line, which was parading up and down merely to show its speed, was seen coming down upon them like lightning . . . Lord W—— saved his life only by rushing behind the duke's carriage . . ., while poor Mr. Huskisson, less active from the effects of age and ill health, bewildered, too, by the frantic cries of 'Stop the engine! Clear the track!' that resounded on all sides, completely lost his head . . . and was instantaneously prostrated by the fatal machine, which dashed down like a thunderbolt upon him, and passed over his leg, smashing and mangling it in the most horrible way . . . Lord W—— was the first to raise the poor sufferer, and calling to aid his surgical skill, which is considerable, he tied up the severed artery . . . Mr. Huskisson was then placed in a carriage with his wife and Lord W—, and the engine, having been detached from the directors' carriage, conveyed them to Manchester. So great was the shock produced upon the whole party by this event, that the Duke of Wellington declared his intention not to proceed, but to return immediately to Liverpool. However, upon its being represented to him that the whole population of Manchester had turned out to witness the procession, and that a disappointment might give rise to riots and disturbances, he consented to go on, and gloomily enough the rest of the journey was accomplished. . . . Lord W—— did not return till past ten o'clock, at which hour he brought the intelligence of Mr. Huskisson's death."

The day ended with a number of minor accidents in pouring rain. But the success of the railway had been proved.

NOVELTY AND TRAIN

North Star and Train

RAILWAY BUILDING

THE Liverpool and Manchester Railway was an immediate success. Passengers flocked to travel on it and made up its principal traffic for the first few years. Goods traffic, which its proprietors had supposed would bring in the bulk of the receipts, was overshadowed. Promoters of trunk lines such as The London and Birmingham, The Grand Junction (Birmingham to Warrington) and The Great Western (London to Bristol) were encouraged to apply to Parliament for powers to build railways.

Before a Bill could be presented in Parliament, plans of the proposed railway had to be deposited. The surveyors had no powers to enter private property, so they often had to work under great difficulties. Farmers loosed bulls on them, and gamekeepers with guns sometimes patrolled estates which the line must cross. Difficult as it was, the survey was only the beginning of the battle. Before a Bill could become an Act, opposition from landowners often had to be bought off by paying huge compensation. (Landowners did exceptionally well. Not only did the railway when built almost invariably increase the value of their holdings, but they were paid compensation for a supposed loss as well.) Some would only withdraw their objections when expensive and circuitous deviations had been agreed. For example, the Earls of Essex and Clarendon forced The London and Birmingham Railway to spend thousands of pounds to avoid their estates by taking the railway through a deep cutting, across the Colne Valley on an embankment and through a long tunnel. Canals and turnpikes sometimes imposed almost impossible conditions before allowing their property to be bridged. Universities and Colleges objected to railways altogether, and often forced them to build a station far from the centre of a town. The Eton authorities had a clause inserted in the Great Western Act, stipulating that no station should be built even at Slough—a stipulation the Great Western evaded by stopping its trains at Slough without building a platform, and arranging for tickets to be sold at a nearby public house. Cort warned that, by improving travel to the Continent, "English teachers at Eton and elsewhere must give way to French governesses assisted not by masters but by mistresses. Homer, Virgil, Horace and other authors—with the single exception of Ovid's 'Art of Love'—will be forced into the background in order that Rousseau, Voltaire, and other equally insinuating and scarcely less destructive writers may be thrust into the foreground." The Duke of Wellington opposed railways "because they would encourage the lower classes to move about." The inhabitants of Brompton required the Great Western to approach London on a viaduct twenty feet high topped by a six-foot parapet to prevent the passengers overlooking them. Dr. Dionysius Lardner said that the Box Tunnel was dangerous and unpractical since passengers passing through it would become nervous wrecks.

The new railways were also violently attacked in some sections of the press. *John Bull* wrote :

> "Does anybody mean to say that decent people, passengers who would use their own carriages . . . would consent to be hurried along through the air upon a railroad . . .; or is it to be imagined that women . . . would endure the fatigue, and misery, and danger . . . of being dragged through the air at the rate of twenty miles an hour, all their lives being at the mercy of a tin pipe, or a copper boiler, or the accidental dropping of a pebble on the line of way?
>
> We denounce the mania as destructive of the country in a thousand particulars—the whole face of the Kingdom is to be tattooed with these odious deformities—huge mounds are to intersect our beautiful valleys; the noise and stench of locomotive steam-engines are to disturb the quietude of the peasant, the farmer and the gentleman . . .
>
> Railroads . . . will in their efforts to gain ground do incalculable mischief. If they succeed they will give an unnatural impetus to society, destroy all the relations which exist between man and man, overthrow all mercantile regulations, overturn the metropolitan markets, drain the provinces of all their resources, and create, at the peril of life, all sorts of confusion and distress."

For all these reasons and many more, the Committee stage of railway Bills was often interminable and parliamentary expenses enormous. The London and Birmingham Railway alone spent over £70,000 before it obtained its Act. Isambard Kingdom Brunel (1806-1859), engineer of the Great Western, was on one occasion cross-examined for eleven days. Serjeant Mereweather, who conducted the opposition to the second Great Western Bill, wound up his case with a speech lasting four days. But the opposition could not stop the railways; it could only delay them. Public need and public demand were too great to be put off.

THE ATMOSPHERIC RAILWAY AT DAWLISH, 1847
Unsigned water colour

THE METROPOLITAN RAILWAY NEAR PADDINGTON, 1863
Lithograph printed in colours

The great main lines could never have been built at this time save for the mass of labour that was available. The population of the cities had grown faster than the factories which had created them. There was poverty and unemployment all over the country. To employers of the time, the man-made laws of supply and demand seemed as immutable as Newton's laws of motion. Combinations of the workers to secure higher wages seemed an interference with the laws of God and were ruthlessly put down. So it was that the railways were able to make tens of thousands of men work for low wages under conditions unequalled since the Pharaohs.

If the engineering works of the new railways were huge, the engineering methods used were relatively simple, though stationary pumping engines were often installed for draining tunnels and cuttings, locomotives were used to some extent for haulage, and rock was attacked with gunpowder. But, broadly speaking, the first railways were built, as the Pyramids had been built, by the labour of men. John Britton, writing in Bourne's *London and Birmingham Railway* (1839), described the making of an embankment at Boxmoor thus:

"The horse, in moving along the top of the embankment, draws the rope attached to a wheelbarrow round two pulleys, and thereby raises the barrow of earth up the sloping board, together with the labourer who holds and guides it. This is a dangerous occupation, for the man rather hangs to, than supports the barrow, which is rendered unmanageable by the least irregularity in the horse's motion. If he finds himself unable to govern it, he endeavours, by a sudden jerk, to raise himself erect; then, throwing the barrow over one side of the board, or 'run,' he swings himself round and runs down the other. Should both fall on the same side, his best speed is necessary to escape the barrow, which, with its contents, comes bounding down after him. Although there were from thirty to forty horse-runs in the Tring cutting constantly working, during many months . . ., and each labourer was precipitated down the slopes several times; such, from continual practice, was their sure-footedness, that only one fatal accident occurred. A moving platform was invented by the engineer to supersede the necessity of thus risking life and limb, but the workmen, who considered it was designed to lessen their labour and wages, broke it."

Dickens described the building of the great cutting from Camden Town to Euston in *Dombey and Son*:

"Houses were knocked down; streets broken through and stopped; deep pits and trenches dug in the ground; enormous heaps of earth and clay thrown up; buildings that were undermined and shaking, propped by great beams of wood. Here, a chaos of carts, overthrown and jumbled together, lay topsy-turvy at the bottom of a steep unnatural hill; there, confused treasures of iron soaked and rusted in something that had

TRING CUTTING, JUNE 17th, 1837

accidentally become a pond. Everywhere were bridges that led nowhere; thoroughfares that were wholly impassable; Babel towers of chimneys, wanting half their height; temporary wooden houses and enclosures, in the most unlikely situations; carcasses of ragged tenements, and fragments of unfinished walls and arches, and piles of scaffolding, and wilderness of bricks, and giant forms of cranes, and tripods straddling above nothing. There were a hundred thousand shapes and substances of incompleteness, wildly mingled out of their places, upside down, burrowing in the earth, aspiring in the air, mouldering in the water, and unintelligible as any dream. Hot springs and fiery eruptions . . . lent their contributions of confusion to the scene. Boiling water hissed and heaved within dilapidated walls; whence also, the glare and roar of flames came issuing forth; and mounds of ashes blocked up rights of way, and wholly changed the law and custom of the neighbourhood.

In short, the yet unfinished and unopened railroad was in progress; and from the very core of all this dire disorder, trailed smoothly away, upon its mighty course of civilisation and improvement."

Of the early main lines, the Great Western was one of the most remarkable. Within a fortnight of the passing of its Act in 1835, Brunel persuaded the directors to allow him to make the distance between the rails seven foot instead of the usual four foot eight and a half inches. (He

PUMPS FOR DRAINING THE KILSBY TUNNEL, c. 1837

had purposely left out any mention of the gauge in the Act.) He considered that the West Country would be the exclusive preserve of the Great Western, and that almost all traffic would be to and from London. North and South traffic would be negligible so the break of gauge would be unimportant. Alternatively, he argued that all other railways would sooner or later have to be altered to meet his new standard, for he thought the broad gauge would mean faster, more comfortable and safer travel. Brunel laid out the best main line in Britain, with few curves, and almost level except for two gradients at Wootton Bassett and through the Box Tunnel.

The Great Western was opened throughout its length in 1841. Within three years the difficulties of a break of gauge had become acute. The line from Bristol to Gloucester was broad gauge, from Gloucester on to Birmingham narrow gauge. Passengers and goods had to be transhipped at Gloucester, which was in a state of permanent confusion, encouraged as much as possible by the narrow gauge party who wished to prove that the broad gauge was a failure. (The broad gauge party argued that the transhipment caused little if any delay.) When representatives of a Parliamentary Committee dealing with gauge problems visited Gloucester, two trains which had already been loaded were unloaded again, and the visitors "were appalled by the clamor arising from well arranged confusion of shouting out addresses of consignments, the chucking of packages across from truck to

Bath Station, 1846

truck, the enquiries for missing articles, the loading, unloading, and reloading . . ." Finally the narrow gauge party bought up the broad gauge line from Gloucester to Bristol and thus decisively defeated the broad gauge, which lingered on till 1892.

Brunel did not stop at the broad gauge. He adopted a system of power different from anything which had been used before when he laid out the South Devon Railway. This was the atmospheric system, by which trains were hauled by a piston running in a pipe laid between the lines. The air in front of the piston was exhausted by pumping installations built at intervals along the line, and the piston with its train was sucked forward. The atmospheric railway had some of the advantages of an electric railway, with a central source of power, the possibility of a dense service of trains, and no smoke or dust. But it also had fatal disadvantages. The piston inside the pipe had to be attached to the train outside the pipe. To do this, the pipe had a slit from end to end through which an arm projected from the piston. The slit was sealed in front and behind by a leather flap which opened to allow the arm to pass. This was a failure. The flap could not be kept airtight because the leather perished. Rats attacked it. Water collected in the pipe. The atmospheric railway had to be abandoned with a loss of hundreds of thousands of pounds.

ENTRANCE TO LOCOMOTIVE ENGINE HOUSE, CAMDEN TOWN, c. 1838

Brunel was one of the greatest engineers of the nineteenth century, imaginative if megalomaniac, bold and direct, an individualist who worked himself to death because he would not delegate the detail of his work to his assistants.

He died in 1859 just after completing one of his greatest railway works, still one of the great monuments of Britain—the Saltash Bridge over the Tamar estuary, west of Plymouth. The *Morning Chronicle* summed him up in its obituary:

> "The history of invention records no instance of grand novelties so boldly imagined and so successfully carried out by the same individual. He was less successful when he was less bold . . . Brunel could make an engineering epic, but not an engineering sonnet. When he could not be grand he was nothing at all. Fortunately, both for himself and the country, he lived at the very period of all others when speculative undertakings had at the same time the most need and the greatest scope for grand ideas. His career forms an epoch in British enterprise upon which he has left the impress . . . of his own mind. He has made it more colossal, but less shapely; and in all probability it will be left to inferior minds to turn to profitable account the conception of a genius who did not always stop to reason, and very seldom to calculate."

Brunel and the other engineers were given a free hand by the shareholders, for the economy of Britain in the mid-nineteenth century was an expanding one. Money was plentiful and, equally important, there was an enthusiasm which was rarely curbed by considerations of mere economy, and which has not been equalled since save in America and Russia. The railway makers were sure of themselves, and convinced that their works had to be the finest of their kind; they felt that they were building, not for the profit of the shareholders alone, but for Britain and the world. Britton, justifying Philip Hardwick's magnificent arch at the entrance of Euston, said, "Objections have been made, and with some appearance of reason, to the great expense of this ornamental entrance: in reply to which, it may be said that, the Railway is a great national undertaking, and that the national character is, in some respects, involved in the execution of the whole." "Centuries hence," said Roscoe, an early railway historian, "when with few, very few, exceptions, even the deeds as well as the names of the heroes, the conquerors, and the politicians of the present day will have become engulfed in one common oblivion, those of Watt and Stephenson will be found rolling imperishably down the stream of time, and fertilising the whole habitable globe with the magnificent creations of their genius." And again, "*The Grand Junction Railway* will ever maintain its importance in the great undertakings of this country. It can afford to smile with complacency upon schemes of more gigantic comprehension or costly expenditure, while it points to the complete demonstration it has afforded to science . . ., and the almost boundless impulse it has mainly contributed to give to the talent, industry, enterprise, and inventive faculties of the world."

Such was the spirit of the railway builders. They brought in the finest architects of their day and the finest engineers. Their works will one day be seen to have contributed to one of the great architectural periods in British history. Most people still do not see the strength which the railways have given to the British landscape. The noble viaducts and bridges seem an intrusion. The solid finely planned station buildings, whether for a country town, or a city, have lost their outline in the imagination. Even the railway companies daub advertisements on Brunel's great viaduct across Chippenham, and impertinently place an enquiry booth in Hardwick's great room in Euston—one of the best interiors of the nineteenth century. Perhaps one day we shall come back to the freshness of vision which made Roscoe write of a viaduct over the Rea near Birmingham, "This magnificent erection is built on a curve of sixty chains radius, exhibiting the graceful contour of a crescent, and may challenge a comparison with any of the works of ancient and modern art both for the impregnable strength of its structure, and the flowing line of beauty it exhibits as it bends gracefully from the massy town to which it is connected, into all the beauty and verdure of the country that lies before."

"Mind Your Points" 1867

THE RAILWAYS SPREAD

THE change which the railways brought to the people of Britain was enormous, and happening in so short a space of time, perhaps had an effect more stunning than any social or economic or technical change before or since. Within fifteen years the ways of life of the people were altered. Millions travelled who had never travelled before. Without railways the mass distribution of cheap literature would have been impossible. The eating habits of the cities changed, for the price of meat fell, and fresh vegetables were within reach of most city dwellers for the first time. The railways quickly became the greatest single employer in the country. They created the British export trade of the nineteenth century by making it possible to transport goods cheaply to the docks. They revolutionised methods of government by making Members of Parliament hours instead of days away from their constituencies. They transformed agriculture.

With the good they brought, evil came too. For the railways became the tightest monopoly Britain has ever known. In spite of protests in every paper and in the Houses of Parliament, their position was such that they neglected improvement, for the only incentive the nineteenth century knew was the incentive of competition, and for the railways there was no competition possible at this time.

The railways killed nearly all long distance road travel, and bought up every canal they could cajole or compel to sell out to them. They destroyed thousands of miles of waterway to the permanent detriment of the country, as anyone can see to-day who compares the flourishing Grand Union Canal from London to Birmingham which has remained independent, with the derelict Kennet and Avon Canal, from London to Bristol, bought and neglected by The Great Western Railway for nearly a hundred years.

The railways did not reach their secure position without troubles. People objected to the smoke and noise of the steam locomotive for many years, and an injunction was even served against one Northern line which successfully prevented the use of locomotives for some weeks. Many objected to Sunday travel, and a Northumberland clergyman distributed the following notice when he heard of a Sunday trip advertised by The Newcastle and Carlisle Railway:

A Reward for Sabbath Breaking.
People taken safely and swiftly to Hell!
Next Lord's Day, by the Carlisle Railway, for 7s. 6d.
It is a Pleasure Trip!

And, week by week, *John Bull*, the greatest railway hater of all, kept up an embittered chronicle of railway accidents and railway inefficiencies. In 1848 it said:

CANNON STREET STATION, C. 1900
Illustration by Marcus from an unidentified periodical

CAMDEN TOWN ENGINE SHEDS, c. 1935
L.M.S. poster by Norman Wilkinson

"The whole system of railroading is conspiracy. The speculators conspire to buy coaches off the turn-pike roads, in order to ensure exclusive power, in a most disgraceful manner—they conspire to conceal the accidents which occur upon their odious speculations; insolence growing out of growing monopoly, characterises the conduct of their servants; while in the performance of their contracts with their passengers, their constant failures bring the uncertainty of their unnatural speed rather below the level of the good steady ten miles an hour pace of English travelling, which, with good English horses, and good English roads, such as ours were (the pride and envy of Europe), would send any man—except an escaping murderer, or a self-liberated felon—quite as fast across a country as he need desire to go."

There was some justice in John Bull's accusations, for accidents were common. This was partly because of the wretched wages many of the men earned (a twelve hour day, seven days a week, for a wage of anything from 15/- to 25/- a week was no exception), and partly due to lack of rules. On one railway, where it was necessary for the engine to be transferred from the front to the back of the train, the driver would uncouple his engine when in motion, steam ahead of the train rolling along under its own momentum, divert his engine into a loop, alter the points, and allow the train to run past. Sir Daniel Gooch (1816-1889), Locomotive Engineer on the Great Western, described another hair-raising experience:

"Only one line of rails was complete through the [Box] tunnel the day we opened, and the trains had therefore to be worked on a single line. I undertook to accompany all the trains through the tunnel . . . I was going up the tunnel with the last up-train, when I fancied I saw some green lights placed as they were in front of our trains. A second's reflection convinced me it was the mail coming down. I lost no time in reversing the engine I was on and running back to Box Station with my train as quickly as I could, when the mail came down behind me. The policeman at the top of the tunnel had made some blunder. . ."

Signals were often merely coloured discs on the top of poles which were turned edge on to the train when the line was clear. Flags alone were often used, with lights at night. Until signal boxes were connected by telegraph, trains followed one another after a given interval of time, the drivers being warned to keep a look out for a train in front in case it had got into difficulties. Even as late as 1881, a train held up in a tunnel on The Great Northern Railway near King's Cross was run into successively by no less than three following trains which had been sent forward, though the telegraph had been installed for some years.

Travelling was as uncomfortable as it was dangerous. Though a Royal Saloon might be a sort of upholstered drawing-room on wheels, even first class passengers had to travel boxed up in carriages modelled on horse coaches, without light at night save for a smelly, dripping oil lamp in the roof, without heating save for foot-warmers, without any means of communicating with the next compartment or the guard (alarm cords were not fitted until quite late and were made compulsory after a murder in a compartment), without means of feeding except by a rush to the refreshment room at a big station (jokes about railway food and buns go back to 1845), without being allowed to smoke anywhere on the train, and made seasick by a motion which—on The York and North Midland Railway at least—was "almost like the rolling of a ship at sea and went far to produce a similar unpleasant climax."

Second class carriages usually had roofs but were not enclosed at the sides. Third class passengers, if they were carried at all, travelled in trucks often without even a roof, and sometimes without seats. This was not put right till 1844, when a law was passed compelling all railways to put roofs on third class carriages and to run at least one train for third class passengers each weekday, stopping at each station on each line.

Neither accidents, discomforts, parliamentary expenses, nor abuse could stop the railways booming. By 1840 gambling in railway shares had begun. New railway schemes were started every day. Some were sensible, but more had no sense in them, the promoters launching them only in order to sell the shares at a premium. By 1845 Britain had gone railway mad. Shares, often of companies which never could have had any hope of success and of which the routes had never even been surveyed, were sold and resold, and sold again. The amount of money invested was far greater than the real value of all the undertakings and proposals put together. In January, 1845, sixteen new companies were registered, in February more than thirty, in March more than fifty. Later in the year, *The Manchester Guardian* calculated that three hundred and fifty-seven projected railways with an aggregate capital of £332,000,000 had been advertised in one month alone.

The Railway Mania—as this period was called—produced one of the first millionaire swindlers. This was George Hudson (1800-1871), the 'Railway King,' a linen draper of York, who inherited a fortune. From 1833 to 1845 he gradually gained control of hundreds of miles of line, principally in the Midlands and on the North East Coast. He amalgamated companies. He sold one to another. He floated new companies to buy up old ones. He doubled dividends by drawing on capital. He raised capital for one company and used it to cover revenue losses of another. Shareholders were dazed by his manipulations but, consoled by bigger and bigger dividends, supported him in all he did.

In twelve years he made an enormous fortune. He bought a house in Albert Gate. He entertained on a prodigious scale. He was shrewd, arrogant and vain. He was a harsh employer, though he also sometimes did odd, sporadic acts of generosity. Yet, for all his swindles, he had vision. He

Queen Victoria, The Prince Consort and Louis Philippe in the Royal Carriage, 1844

believed passionately in railways, and it was through his efforts that The North Eastern Railway became one of the best-planned and largest railways in Britain.

George Hudson's prosperity and the wild railway speculation from 1845 to 1849 did not last. Early in 1849, when railway shares were already slumping, it was discovered that Hudson had sold shares which he owned in one company to another company he controlled at a price above market quotation. Committees of enquiry were set up. Hudson was forced to resign from directorship after directorship. The railway share market collapsed and thousands of people were ruined. But Hudson was never brought into court for embezzlement; too many people would have been involved. Indeed, when he was found to be very poor in 1868, the Conservative party in Sunderland bought him an annuity of £600 a year, and he was re-elected chairman of the smoking room of the Carlton Club.

The pricking of the 'Railway Bubble' checked speculation in railway shares and the fraudulent promotion of unsound schemes, but it did not stop the railways quarrelling among themselves. As the main lines were extended, railways began to fight each other. Railway Bills came to be

THE GREAT RAILWAY GUY OF 1849

opposed, not by canals (which could compete no longer) or by landowners (who had long since realised that nearly every railway was an asset) but by other railways. The London and York Railway, The Direct Northern Railway, The Eastern Counties Railway and other groups spent over £500,000 in Parliament between them, contesting for the line from London to York which was finally built under the title of The Great Northern Railway.

The London and North Western Railway fought the Great Western Railway's extensions towards Wolverhampton and Chester. The Great Northern fought the Manchester, Sheffield and Lincoln's plan for a new line to London. The Manchester, Sheffield and Lincoln fought the Great Northern's plan to tap coalfields in the Midlands. The Midland Railway fought them both. The struggles were not only parliamentary. Junctions were torn up, and there were even battles between rival parties of gangers and navvies. When one railway obtained running powers over another, their trains might be held up and delayed. Time-tables were drawn up to prevent connections being made between rival systems.

In spite of squabbles and fights, litigation and speculation, the railway system spread. Many of the main lines of to-day were either built or building by the fifties. The last great gaps were filled in by degrees by tunnels and bridges which are enduring engineering and architectural masterpieces. The Menai Strait was bridged in 1850 and the Tyne in 1849 by Robert Stephenson. The Tamar was bridged by Brunel in 1859. The Severn Tunnel was opened in 1886 and The Forth Bridge, the last great piece of British railway engineering and the finest of them all, in 1890.

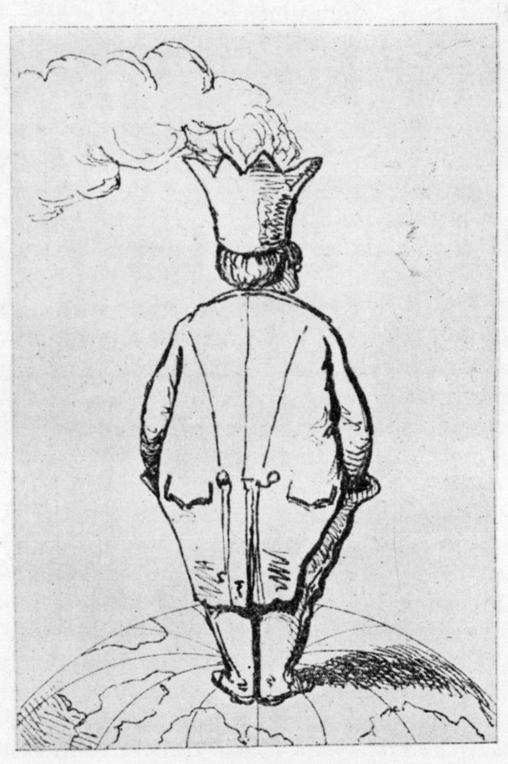

THE RAILWAY KING

UNDERGROUND

IN cities, such as London, the interchange of goods and passengers between terminus and terminus was difficult. London streets, paved with cobbles, were choked by horse buses, carriages and carts. The streets were filthy. The noise of the ironshod wheels on the cobbles was deafening. For, by the middle of the nineteenth century, it was estimated that about quarter of a million passengers used the London termini each day.

Charles Pearson, a London solicitor, seems to have been the first man to suggest that the stations could be linked up by an underground line. His suggestion for some reason became a music hall joke. A Doctor Cummings suggested an overhead railway instead, to be covered by a glass roof and to be called the "Crystal Way." Another suggestion was that the Regent's Canal should be drained and used for a railway. However, overground railways, at least in central London, were out of the question. They had to be built underground or not built at all. The objections to underground railways were two. Ventilation would be difficult, and the work of underpinning London's buildings complicated and expensive. Though the latter difficulty could have been met by boring deep tunnels far below the foundations, it would have been impossible to ventilate them. So long as steam was used, railway tunnels had to be made near the surface, so that there could be frequent vents to the open air.

The engineer, John Fowler (1817-1898), reported in favour of a railway near the surface from Bishop's Road, near Paddington, to Farringdon Street, connecting Paddington, Euston, St. Pancras, Kings Cross and the terminus of the Eastern Counties Railway which had not yet been brought into the city.

Powers were granted by Parliament in 1853, but work did not start till 1860. The Metropolitan Railway was built in under three years. It followed wherever possible the line of a street, which was opened up by building a great trench down the centre. This was roofed and the street relaid. Watermains and gas mains had to be moved, and the River Fleet had to be diverted into a huge steel pipe. While this was being done, the Fleet sewer burst, and the works were flooded. All these difficulties were overcome, and on January 9th, 1863, a banquet was given at Farringdon Street, and the Cabinet with Mr. Gladstone were drawn along the railway sitting in an open truck. Next day the railway was opened to the public, and carried 30,000 passengers. Nearly 10,000,000 people were carried in the first year, and by 1870 the number of passengers using the railway was over 180,000,000.

Travelling on The Metropolitan was uncomfortable. The tunnels were filled with sulphurous smoke. The carriages were lighted by oil lamps which smelled, dripped and flickered. Gas, held in long rubber bags on the tops of the carriages, was not much of an improvement, and passengers who

THE METROPOLITAN RAILWAY, 1872

wanted to read often stuck candles on to the sides of the compartments. And every crack in every building was put down to the trains. Said *Punch* :

I thunder down to work each morn
And some historic shrine
Must have its matchless fabric torn
To get me there at nine.

And when I gather up my traps
As sundown sets me free
A nation's monuments collapse
To take me home to tea.

It became obvious that London's traffic problems could not be completely solved by underground railways near the surface. The disorganisation of the streets while they were being built was very great; they had more or less to follow the direction of streets; and the engineering works when they had to be taken through congested areas, such as the City, were prohibitively expensive. Accordingly, the first deep level tube railways date back almost to the first Metropolitan line. Peter Barlow and James Henry Greathead invented a 'shield' which gnawed into the London clay, and built The Tower Tunnel under the Thames in 1870. It was only seven feet in diameter but it was lined with cast iron sections like a modern tube. The gauge of the railway was only two foot six inches, and the carriages were drawn by a rope. It was closed in 1894 when the Tower Bridge was opened.

The first of the modern tubes was The City and South London from Stockwell to King William Street. The power system was to have been an endless cable which would be gripped by the carriages. (The Glasgow Subway used this system till well after the 1914-1918 war.) Before the railway was opened in 1890 the engineers decided to drive the trains by electric locomotives. The first carriages had no windows, and were hot and airless.

Other tube railways were soon built. The Waterloo and City Railway was opened in 1898; The Central London Railway—the 'Twopenny Tube'—from Shepherd's Bush to the Bank in 1900. The Metropolitan and Metropolitan District Railways were soon electrified, and both these and the tubes were gradually extended till they crossed London from end to end, and ran far out into the home counties. To-day the underground railways, the buses and the trams have all been absorbed into one undertaking—The London Passenger Transport Board.

On the Continent

THE TWENTIETH CENTURY

BY 1900 the railway network in Britain—nearly 50,000 miles of it—was substantially what it is to-day. The last of the main lines to reach London, The Great Central, was opened to Marylebone in 1899, though the Great Western had not completed all the short cuts to straighten out its routes to Plymouth, South Wales and Birmingham. Indeed, few new lines could have been laid out, for Britain already had one of the densest railway networks in the world, because of the competitive and haphazard way in which the lines had been planned. (This railway profligacy has been unexpectedly useful. There are so many alternative routes that it is difficult to paralyse British railways by air attack. The French railways, mainly built under planned schemes by which duplication was avoided, are much more vulnerable.)

Accordingly, from 1900 till now the railways have worked mainly within limits laid down in the nineteenth century. The distance between the lines and, of much greater importance, the "loading gauge," which determines the overall size of locomotives and rolling stock in relation to the size of tunnels and the clearance of overbridges and platforms, were both laid down a hundred years ago. It is fortunate that early locomotives had tall chimneys to keep up a good draught to the fire and projecting cranks and cylinders. These compelled the railway builders to allow plenty of room in tunnels and on bridges, so that large modern locomotives can often pass along lines little modified since the time they were laid out perhaps a hundred years ago. Though America has the same rail gauge as Britain, her loading gauge is much more generous and her locomotives are larger and more powerful. Nevertheless, even with the more generous loading gauge of America, the problem of the railway engineer all over the world is to fit more and more powerful designs of locomotive into limits laid down generations ago. To-day, it seems that the conventional steam railway as we know it has nearly reached the end of its development.

What can be called the modern phase of railway practice dates back to about 1875 when competition between the lines forced the various companies to adopt new standards of speed, comfort and safety. Bogie carriages gradually superseded four-wheel and six-wheel carriages. In 1872 the Midland opened all its trains to third class passengers instead of keeping them out of the best and fastest expresses. The Midland's rivals regarded the new move as socialism but followed when they saw that the encouragement of third class travel was profitable. In 1874 the Midland abolished second class and introduced upholstered seats into all third class carriages. The Great Northern brought in sleeping cars in 1873 and the London and North Western in 1874. The Great Northern started dining cars in 1879 and corridor trains were introduced in 1892 by the Great Western. Something not unlike the modern buffet car was introduced by the Great Central in 1899 but did not catch on. Buffet cars were successfully re-introduced by the London and North Eastern in 1932.

The most spectacular aspect of the competition was the railway race to Aberdeen in 1895. The Forth Bridge had been opened for passenger traffic in 1890 and, for the first time, the East Coast route to Aberdeen from King's Cross through Edinburgh could compete with the West Coast route from Euston through Perth. The distance by the former is 523½ miles, by the latter 540 miles. Both routes used the same line from Kinnaber Junction thirty miles into Aberdeen, and whichever train reached Kinnaber first had right of way. At the beginning of 1895, the running time by the former was eleven hours thirty-five minutes, by the latter quarter of an hour longer. Late in June the West Coast Companies cut their running time by ten minutes, and the East Coast knocked quarter of an hour off their schedule in reply. The West Coast route put up posters in Euston announcing that on July 15th the Aberdeen service would come down to eleven hours, and the first train of the new schedule actually covered the 540 miles in ten hours twenty minutes. On July 22nd the East Coast route cut their schedule to ten and three quarter hours. After that the West Coast route ignored the timetable and tried to reach Kinnaber Junction ahead of their rival, come what might. On July 29th the East Coast Companies knocked another twenty minutes off the running time, and on August 16th brought it down to nine hours forty minutes. Finally on August 21st, 1895, the East Coast route ran a train which reached Edinburgh in just over six hours and a quarter, and Aberdeen in just under eight and three quarter hours—times which have only been equalled as normal running in the last eight years. On August 22nd the West Coast did the journey to Aberdeen in just over eight and a half hours at an average speed of just over sixty-seven miles an hour. Next day the race was called off, for the speeds were becoming dangerous, and both main lines had been disorganised.

Another record run was put up by The Great Western Railway in 1904 when competing with The London and South Western Railway for the mail contract to Plymouth. The *City of Truro* is said to have touched over a hundred and two miles an hour near Taunton, and a train ran from Bristol to London in an hour and forty-six minutes at an average speed of about seventy miles an hour. In spite of exceptional times such as these, the average speeds of expresses rarely touched sixty miles an hour, and were commonly less than fifty miles an hour, till well into the twentieth century.

Throughout the second half of the nineteenth century traffic had been increasing. Single lines had to be doubled, double lines to be quadrupled. Trains became heavier. More powerful engines had to be built. Steel instead of iron rails were laid down. Suburban traffic grew year by year. The Great Northern and The Great Eastern had to widen the approaches to

The Arrival Platform at Victoria Station
Oil painting by James Tissot

King's Cross and Liverpool Street at enormous expense. Increased speeds and weights, and denser traffic led to decreased distances between trains, and automatic brakes, operating on each wheel of a train, became essential. At the same time, more powerful and faster locomotives had to be designed.

The prototypes of the locomotives which are familiar to-day mainly had their origin between 1894 and 1905. Between these dates, several of the main lines brought in locomotives with six coupled wheels and a leading

The Forth Bridge

four-wheeled bogie (the 4-6-0), or with four coupled wheels, a four-wheeled bogie and a pair of trailing wheels (the so-called Atlantic or 4-4-2). These new wheel arrangements allowed for longer boilers of greater capacity. At the same time the diameter of the boilers has been gradually increased till to-day they almost fill the limits allowed by the loading gauge. Boiler pressures were increased and, in the 4-4-2 type of engine, it was possible to fit very large fireboxes. Steam was 'superheated'; that is, its temperature was raised by passing it through a system of pipes in direct contact with the hot flue gases from the firebox. All these things led to greater engine power to meet the greater train weights and train speeds.

The first British 4-6-0 was designed by David Jones for goods traffic on The Highland Railway in 1894, and in 1902 William Dean introduced a two-cylinder passenger 4-6-0 on the Great Western which, modified and enlarged, is still the standard to-day, and which has influenced locomotive design on all the other railways. The first 4-4-2 was designed by H. A. Ivatt for the Great Northern in 1898. This type was the ancestor of the 4-6-2 'Pacific' engines, introduced on the Great Northern in 1922, which to-day are the standard express locomotives of The London and North Eastern Railway. *Mallard*, of this type, touched a hundred and twenty-six miles an hour on July 3rd, 1938—a world's record for a steam locomotive. Similar engines worked the King's Cross—Edinburgh expresses in seven hours for the 393 miles with trains weighing up to five hundred tons, or in six hours with specially designed and lighter trains. (The Great Western introduced a Pacific as early as 1908, but its weight and long wheel base prevented its adoption as a standard, and only one—*The Great Bear*—was built. It was converted to a 4-6-0 in 1924.) The London, Midland and Scottish introduced Pacifics in 1933, and the Southern in 1942.

There have been similar changes in locomotives for goods traffic. Where the express engine requires a four-wheeled bogie in front to allow for fast cornering, a goods engine does not need to travel so fast, and most or all of its weight can be concentrated on to its driving wheels without the use of bogies. Accordingly the standard designs of goods engine are usually the 0-6-0, the 0-8-0 and the 2-8-0 (first introduced by the Great Western).

Besides inter-railway competition and increasing loads, another factor began to influence railway practice from about 1900. Till that date the railways had almost a complete monopoly of long distance traffic, except that carried by the canals they had been unable to destroy, and of much short distance traffic. Electric street tramways, first widely introduced in 1895, began to attract short distance passenger traffic and to cut into railway revenues. To meet the new competition, suburban lines round London, Manchester, Liverpool and Newcastle-upon-Tyne, were electrified to give a quick and intensive service. Other railways, such as the Great Northern and the Great Eastern revised their steam services and designed new and powerful tank engines to give quick acceleration and faster speeds between stations.

Finally the war of 1914-1918 proved that railway transport could no longer be handled efficiently by sixteen major and dozens of minor companies, many with separate standards of equipment, rules and systems of signalling. The railways were forced to co-operate by unifying their services and by pooling rolling stock and locomotives. This led directly to the amalgamation on January 1st, 1923, of the railways into four groups—The London, Midland and Scottish, The London and North Eastern, The Great Western (the only railway to keep its identity) and The Southern. These four groups together represent the most powerful single industrial combine in Britain with a combined capital of about £1,000,000,000 and enormous holdings, not only of railways, but of canals, docks, ships, hotels, and road vehicles. The amalgamation led directly to the largest single electrification scheme in the world, that of The Southern Railway, embracing all the suburban traffic and much of the main line traffic of three formerly independent railways.

From 1920, the road-rail war increased in violence because of the growing use of the private car, the motor bus and the motor lorry. The struggle

London & North Western Railway Express, c. 1913

became as fierce, and as damaging to the public, as the inter-railway squabbles of sixty-five years before. Two forms of transport which should have complemented each other tried to destroy each other, and private enterprise seemed incapable of organising them for the common good. Road companies ran services deliberately to undercut parallel railway services. The railways threatened to revive obsolete laws to prevent vehicles of more than a certain weight using many of their overbridges.

Yet railways and roads are organised in different ways, and each system can give a distinct and essential service to the community. The railways are, and will remain for many years, by far the best way of moving bulk loads between centres of industry or population relatively far apart, or of giving a dense passenger service along routes which thousands of people must travel each day. The roads could never handle the tens of thousands of tons of goods and the hundreds of thousands of passengers delivered each day to London.

Road transport can give a door-to-door and factory-to-factory service which the railways cannot hope to equal. Road transport is ideal for short runs, for small mixed loads to be delivered at many different points, and for connecting small communities with large ones.

Though the road-rail war has been expensive, wasteful and footling, it has at least compelled the railways to introduce many things which were due to the public without the adventitious spur of competition. Compartments were given more comfortable seats and bigger windows. Third class sleepers came in in 1928. Third class return fares came down to a penny a mile in 1934. Goods containers, carried on flat trucks and lifted bodily on to road lorries, helped to overcome transhipment difficulties at loading and unloading points. Finally, and most importantly, passenger train speeds were increased till they equalled, or even exceeded, those of the Aberdeen races of 1895. On September 12th, 1932, the Great Western put on the *Cheltenham Flier*, with an average speed of over seventy miles an hour from Swindon to Paddington—the first schedule of its kind in the world. Since 1935, *The Coronation* from King's Cross and *The Coronation Scot* from Euston have brought down the times to Edinburgh and Glasgow to six, and six and a half, hours respectively. At the same time, stream-lined locomotives and trains have been introduced, with a saving of horse power at high speeds. The Great Western, an exceptionally conservative line, after dressing up one of its standard engines to look like a tin of fancy biscuits, so that the smoke blew into the driver's eyes and the bearings ran hot, gave up stream-lining. Nevertheless, the Great Western crack trains, *Cheltenham Flier* and *The Bristolian*, engined by standard locomotives, were little slower or less efficient than the prinked-up vulgar-looking monsters running North, though their runs were much shorter.

By 1939 Britain had one of the fastest and densest railway services in the world. There were one hundred and ten expresses scheduled daily at over sixty miles an hour and several at over seventy. The steam services in Britain and everywhere else were reaching their limit without new developments such as main line electrification or the use of diesel locomotives. The war stopped developments and solved for the time being the road-rail war, partly because of the shortage of petrol, partly by controlling the two forms of transport impartially. As a consequence, Britain's transport services and her transport workers have done a job which few people believed possible.

For many years almost everyone of all political parties has agreed that the co-ordination between rail and road must be kept up, though people differed as to how this should be done. The Labour Party has decided to nationalise the railways and the roads, and to buy out the shareholders. The Party argues that it would not be possible to have railways controlled by the State and road transport left to develop under private ownership. Each must be regulated in relation to the other. With nationalisation the Labour Party will seek to prove that modern society can find an incentive to efficiency other than the competitive struggle for profit. The prototype of the General Post Office suggests that they will succeed.

MAIN LINE

LOCOMOTIVE ON THE STOCKTON AND DARLINGTON RAILWAY, 1825

AUTHOR'S NOTE

This short account of British railways could not have been written without the work of railway historians who have been studying the subject for a hundred years. It could not have been illustrated without the brilliant contemporary drawings and engravings of such men as T. T. Bury and John C. Bourne, ignored for a hundred years by aesthetes and art historians who have taught that no art can come from the vulgar economic pursuits of common man.

I must make particular acknowledgement to the excellent railway histories of the late C. F. Dendy Marshall, who kindly allowed me to quote a number of excerpts, reproduced by him from early contemporary periodicals. I have also taken one or two excerpts from Lady Celia Noble's *The Brunels, Father and Son* (1938) and W. W. Tomlinson's *The North Eastern Railway* (1914). The section headed *Underground* is based on W. J. Passingham's *The Romance of London's Underground*. I am indebted to the authors and the publishers for permission to use these works, to the Birmingham Reference Library for allowing me to quote from the Boulton and Watt papers, and to the proprietors of *Punch* for the poem on p. 39.

The illustrations are drawn from my collection with the exception of those otherwise acknowledged.

SHORT BIBLIOGRAPHY

GENERAL

John Francis, *History of the English Railway*. 2 vols. 1841

F. S. Williams, *Our Iron Roads*. 1851

Samuel Smiles, *Lives of the Engineers*. 1861

W. W. Tomlinson, *The North Eastern Railway*. 1914

E. J. MacDermot, *History of The Great Western Railway*. 2 vols. 1927

C. F. Dendy Marshall, *The Centenary History of the Liverpool and Manchester Railway*. 1930

C. F. Dendy Marshall, *History of British Railways down to the Year 1830*. 1938

Charles E. Lee, *The Evolution of Railways*. 2nd ed. 1943

Rixon Bucknall, *Our Railway History*. 1944

LOCOMOTIVES

J. G. H. Warren, *A Century of Locomotive Building*. Robert Stephenson & Co. 1923

E. L. Ahrons, *The British Locomotive, 1825-1925*. 1927

C. F. Dendy Marshall, *Two Essays in Early Locomotive History*. 1928